Angel Visits

Angel Visits

Garry Ely

Pindrop Press

Published 2013 by
P_indrop Press
Mallards
Steers Place
Hadlow
Kent

www.pindroppress.com

ISBN 978-0-9573290-2-7

A catalogue record for this book is available from the British Library.

Typeset by P_indrop Press.

Printed and bound in the UK by Lightning Source.

Cover image by MJ Pearce, 2012

Acknowledgements

I would like to thank Carrie Bruce, Chris Davis and Caroline Price.

for Christine
(1953–2010)

Contents

‘a conspiracy of snow’

I

The postcard you sent
of a woman alone, her cup of coffee
untouched;
on the back you wrote:
'How serene she looks'
and wished you could feel like that.

Now there is all the time in the world
before we meet
on a railway platform
like this one
where I will endure the tracks
that join together,
and separate,
the places between us.

II

You have been reading
all evening and when you look up,
your face is full of tears.

In bed, you will dream about the heroine:
her last letter;
how she filled her pockets with stones
and was washed up
somewhere you once visited.

III

Distant from me, you clear the table,
pleased that your hands are occupied.
I try to smile
and would like you to touch me
but I merely stand and watch.

You pause at the window
and look over silent fields,
then wash the cups. Lifting them
from the bowl,
water runs off the palms
of your cold hands.

IV

Nothing is about to happen. Upright shadows
stain the wall:
a single bed remembering an imprint.
You collect your father's few, half-known,
impersonal effects.

Afterwards, you listen to the tape
he secretly recorded
and pick up the clues: his undeluded words;
the surface calm. Losing track,
they implicate you
in their tender expression; followed by silence,
then a click.

V

Our room is rinsed by light.
Reading in these armchairs that face each other,
we do not look as the hours darken
this December afternoon that seeps away from us.
Lying round,
objects that we chose together.

Near the television,
a black and white school photograph:
in your final year,
fragile paper sculpture
pinned to your uniform.

You are smiling as if you have nothing to fear.

VI

Drowsy Grasmere is quiet and blurred by mist
as we walk together down the lane
and pause on a narrow wooden bridge.

You tell me to listen
and I hear ice
melt from the empty trees and splash on the water below.
We watch the stream
pacify the multiplying ripples.
Then we walk on: up the other side of the valley
under a blue sky
that widens all around us.

VII

On the radio, a pop song we used to play
obsessively. In love,
lost to it,
you leave your suitcase in the spare room,
spilling letters, underwear,
a pair of earrings.
You cannot stay still.

I bought you that CD.
'She has a halo'
you sing. 'We really do adore her.'

VIII

Mother and daughter and not quite father
watching a repeat of 'The Saint':
this derelict character was murdered in his flat;
a friend is blackmailed and the trusted lawyer
turns out to be the Scorpion.

The evidence against me accumulates.
He's finally tracked down
and cornered.

I always liked that moment
when the Saint looks up expectantly,
waiting for his halo to appear,
knowing he is right.

IX

Your daughter ghosts the length of your mind
in jeans and T-shirt
and swears that she's not going home.
Where does it come from:
this sadness at two or three or four a.m.?

X

Is this you pushing the swing back and forth?

We're in a garden and you overhear:
'He's out of control.'
This impatient child, abandoned by his father,
cannot speak. A magic path
across the civilised expanse of lawn
discovers a hidden sandpit
which he's found and does not want to leave.

The moment is lost to him.
He'll grow older.
They will confiscate his bucket and spade.

XI

You are with me
at my father's graveside.

If he could hear,
I'd like to turn the subject
back to football: Rivelino, Gérson, Tostão;
that impossible lob by Pelé
inside his own half. He drifted the ball out of nowhere.
I can imagine it there and wish that
this time, as it begins to drop,
he will not miss.

XII

You awoke to a conspiracy of snow:
white cells descending
and ascending.
They suffocate the window.

'Wouldn't it be good to walk the hills
and lakes and bookshop again, and we will.
I love you.'

From Dove Cottage
you'd like us to follow the old coffin road until
exhausted, ailing,
you halt at the resting stone. We phone the hospital.
The black mobile
held to your face
interrogates a mouth, an ear.

‘something is happening’

XIII

You unknot your hands and reveal
your small fingers.
One seems inflamed; almost surely from sorrow and love.

As you let me touch them, I feel your fingertips glance
against mine
before they disappear into the palest mauve,
thin gloves.

XIV

Something is happening.
You descend the stairs
backwards,
apologising in a low voice;
each chained step
follows mine.

Returning to the car,
you bury yourself
unobtrusively
at the back,
refusing to hold me responsible.

XV

As I go over it again,
you close your eyes. You don't know where to turn
and cold, confused,
you listen to my voice rise
but do not speak.

You sit on the stairs, wondering how my voice,
now calling your name,
has come between us.
Your mouth suffers as I reach out
and take your hand.
I wish I could give you back my touch.

XVI

Vacant, capsized,
you try one or two steps
and say, 'You are marvellous.'
Your hand stays on my shoulder.
I edge you across the floor,
absorbed in a half-embrace.

The lingering slow motion
is the most that we can hope for;
and learning how to walk
at your own pace.

XVII

Ritually feeding you with bread and soup; important,
precious recipe you taught me.

Your patient mouth opens and shuts
as you wait for more
until there's nothing left.

XVIII

I drive you to the hospital and cannot
bring you back.
I keep the lights on in the house as if
you had never left
but are wandering through the rooms upstairs
and looking at your books.

Imagining I can hear your car pull up,
I tidy the room as if
I had invited you here,
then go out to meet you in the rain.
Your face,
invisible behind the streaming glass.

‘but words perplex you’

XIX

I turn the pages searching for a photograph
of the girl he wrote his poems for;
isolated, inflicting loneliness on himself.

Mourning him, I look into your absent face
and repeat his perfect words
as if I believe they could make ours true.

XX

In the cellar, your old wedding album.
You barely ate for weeks until you could fit
into your dress.

Now it holds you there and seems to tighten
at your throat, your wrists.

XXI

Tonight I come across a novel. Someone has written
behind the cover: 'With love for a happy ending'
(there is also a sad one)
as if it were still possible.

The real one is unravelling without me.

XXII

This afternoon
your disarray is more pronounced,
more painful.

You talk about yourself
in the third person
as if you flinch at events that happened years ago
and are not over yet:
unspoken violence at your convent school;
a loveless marriage.

But words perplex you.
The out of order syllables escape
from one side of your mouth,
beyond recovery.

XXIII

From your sickroom
we can hear the waiting car close by.
The engine dies.

Incurious,
condemned, you go on staring at the broken shapes
your clothes make in the shadows,
preparing to give themselves away.

XXIV

Confined by this catastrophe:
manoeuvring meticulously down the corridor
into the past,
you pause from time to time
and sift your own experience.

Behind you,
a rearrangement of dust;
an implacable disturbance
in the air.

XXV

The ward's competing voices overwhelm you.
I watch you find a paper tissue.

Your hand unfolds the delicate material
and presses it
against your lips.
You cannot alter your slow, solitary
trespass on the future.

XXVI

Listening to the silence, everything is revealed
by your expression. You must eat this loneliness,
chew it each day
and swallow.
'I don't want to die. There's too much to live for.'

You ask why you're still here
and try to force
these narrow wheels across the carpet's crust.

XXVII

Your hand, too weak by itself,
held up with wires
that grow out of it,
leading in one direction.

Against your will,
they have moved you into position
to receive a visitor
whose voice you almost recognise.
As you tire of your dream speech,
I whisper my name.

You repeat it back to me:
an inarticulate code I cannot break or bear.

'we eavesdrop on your voice'

XXVIII

As if we could escape from this:
where they all speak together
fatally, confidingly,
I follow you into your room.
It's taking its course;
your dreams of going back
extinguished.

Watching you fall asleep, as I did yesterday
and all the days before,
I'll wait for you to speak
in your dead voice.
It could be true or an invention.
There isn't a choice.

These anonymous lives, their voice-overs
and asides, are part of ours now.
None of us is able to depart.

XXIX

You cannot raise yourself
and I lift you, unprotesting,
bemused,
giving your permission
but unable to refuse.

'There isn't even a little hope.
I don't want to be a burden.'

Gripping my arm,
you try to move:
performing for me
this forlorn dance
on the spot;
attending to a silent music of confusion.

XXX

Surrendering to the tubes and straps,
you listen to an audio book at maximum volume
and close your eyes.

All I can hear is this inscrutable static:
a stream of unconsciousness.

XXXI

Your fingers deftly touch my sleeve, my collar.
'You've put on a new shirt.
It won't make me change my mind.
I've said goodbye to everyone.'
Although we are alone, you lovingly call out
their names and wave at each of them in turn:
a last glimpse.

One by one, helpless,
resigned,
you let them go.

XXXII

You are in a slow panic;
your body shudders
and then lulls.
This room, which is not your room,
is full of unaccommodating cries
that keep you company.

We eavesdrop on your voice,
slurred to a murmur;
these almost words
enough to tip the scales.
You falter into tears.

Someone has combed your dull hair forwards
and not back.

‘the mysterious succession of days’

XXXIII

Husband and wife, who will not talk of dying,
tread a painful path past flower borders, benches
and through the dead leaves.

You are not here to explain
or make decisions,
nor can you understand the sparse, mundane,
unfluent diction
in this faded leaflet. But you will feel the incision
that's healed over;
the slow pulsing
of what they call a tired heart.

XXXIV

Imprisoned in the pages of a book,
this photograph of a house
we are in love with.
You won't return.

The mysterious succession of days;
their bruised shadows
dissolving.
They say your skin cannot repair itself.

Beyond stillness,
a lifted hand
half-clouds your face:
looking out,
completely unaware of me.

XXXV

You are leaning forward
with your eyes wide open.

Awakening,
you do not move
or make a sound, except for the slight catch
in your breathing
every few seconds
that we will listen out for
through these angel visits
and, in our conversation,
somehow ignore.

XXXVI

Whatever happens, I've found the envelope
resealed, trapped in a drawer,
and the final note that you composed.

I stare at my name: those routine, lacerating details.

XXXVII

Did you know the number of your days?

I'd asked if you could wear the graceful dress you wore
when we were married
eight months ago: a quiet wedding.
It will never be unfastened.

I kiss your mouth
wondering if I might inhale your dove-coloured soul
into my body.

'your absence constantly returns'

XXXVIII

Your face suffuses every room;
in the living room mirror
you are laughing. Your brush is in my hand and I caress
your hair, not mine. My arm crosses
and recrosses your breast.

After your hair grew back,
we thought you looked like Jean Seberg
in 'Breathless'.

The glass clouds over. I'll wait for you to wipe it clean.

XXXIX

This is my dream work:
I wash and iron your clothes; those in our laundry basket;
those from the ward. Your crumpled nightdress
darkened with a dozen drops of blood.

On the ironing board, I lay out these frail, tangible things.
Perhaps they will contain
your last sigh
within their folds
if I could only reassemble them.

XL

I keep your slender bottle of Dior 'Pure Poison'
at my bedside.

Should it be taken
before the light is switched on: between the morning and night;
waking and sleep?

XLI

In the small hours,
invisible,
pressed against your empty place, listening to a voice
that seems to be asking for you;

I overhear it: lost, subdued
and promising not to begin again without you.

XLII

The first day of Christmas and I cannot write
your name on the card
next to mine.

Stilled,
I close my eyes. Once more I'm waiting outside the cinema
and longing for you to appear:
knowing you are never late;
knowing you are keeping
perfect time.

XLIII

In this sanctuary of trees, dark-clustering the pond,
we scatter your ashes. They adhere
to tiny cobwebs and expose
strands of angel hair
which intertwine the brambles, ferns and nettles.

You wished I wouldn't agonise so much.
I trace your tender outline.

XLIV

Now that it's impossible,
I remember when you used to visit
and the unfailing sense remains
that you would like us to meet.
But your absence constantly returns
like light splitting the blinds.

I imagine you climbing out of the car,
a weekend bag tight in your hand,
then watch myself cross the floor
and let you in.

Other poetry titles from Pindrop Press

A Suitable Girl, Michelle McGrane
Pepek the Assassin, Joyce Ellen Davis
Opening the World, Dale Favier
To Know Bedrock, Sharon Black
Snow Child, Abegail Morley
You Do Not Need Another Self-Help Book, Sarah Salway
Last March, Kieran Millwood-Hargrave
Test, Orange, Cherry Smyth
Things That Are Silent, Rethabile Masilo
The Chongololo Club, Graham Burchell
This Instinct Against Death, Emer Gillespie
The Yellow Table, Alicia Stubbersfield
Eva and George — Sketches in Pen and Brush, Abegail Morley

Available from http://www.pindroppress.com

Lightning Source UK Ltd.
Milton Keynes UK
UKOW040613240413

209643UK00001BA/5/P

9 780957 329027